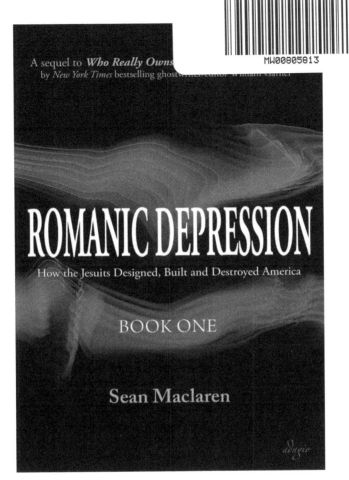

A sequel to *Who Really Owns*
by *New York Times* bestselling ghost

ROMANIC DEPRESSION
How the Jesuits Designed, Built and Destroyed America

BOOK ONE

Sean Maclaren

adagio

Romanic Depression
Available from Amazon.com and
other bookstores

eBook available from Amazon.com, AdagioPress.com and
WilliamDeanAGarner.com

The first book in a four-part series that reveals how the Jesuits have
designed, built and destroyed every sector of American society,
from Law and Government to Politics to Healthcare to Education.
Also with more than 200 excellent references.

Edited by William Dean A. Garner
New York Times bestselling ghostwriter/editor

Burke McCarty

The Suppressed Truth About The Assassination

of *Abraham Lincoln*

The Suppressed Truth
About the Assassination of Abraham Lincoln
Available from Amazon.com and other bookstores

eBook available from Amazon.com, AdagioPress.com and WilliamDeanAGarner.com

Burke McCarty was a courageous ex-Catholic who conducted diligent research on the details surrounding the murder of President Abraham Lincoln by the Jesuits.

Edited by William Dean A. Garner
New York Times bestselling ghostwriter/editor

Machiavelli's *The Prince*
Available from Amazon.com and other bookstores

eBook available from Amazon.com, AdagioPress.com and WilliamDeanAGarner.com

The Prince is a raw and bloody field manual for upper- and mid-level managers on predatorial ethics and power: what it is, how to obtain it, and what to do with it once you have found, stumbled across, or been granted it.

Edited by William Dean A. Garner
New York Times bestselling ghostwriter/editor

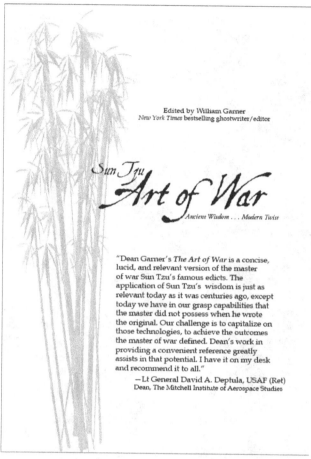

Sun Tzu *The Art of War*
Available from Amazon.com and other bookstores

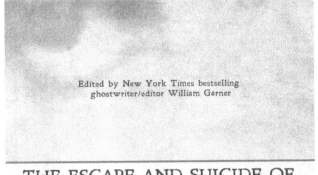

Edited by New York Times bestselling
ghostwriter/editor William Garner

THE ESCAPE AND SUICIDE OF
JOHN WILKES BOOTH
THE JESUIT ASSASSIN OF ABRAHAM LINCOLN

FINIS L. BATES

The Escape and Suicide of
John Wilkes Booth
The Jesuit Assassin of Abraham Lincoln
Available from Amazon.com and
other bookstores

eBook available from Amazon.com, AdagioPress.com and
WilliamDeanAGarner.com

Researcher, author and attorney Finis L. Bates did exhaustive work
to uncover the accurate history about Jesuit assassin John Wilkes
Booth after he murdered President Abraham Lincoln.

Edited by William Dean A. Garner
New York Times bestselling ghostwriter/editor

Fifty Years in the Church of Rome
Available from Amazon.com and other bookstores

eBook available from Amazon.com, AdagioPress.com and
WilliamDeanAGarner.com

Rev. Charles Chiniquy chronicles his 50 years as a servant of the
Church of Rome, while also revealing the evil machinations of the
Jesuits and their Roman Catholic minions. He includes information
about the assassination of President Abraham Lincoln by the Jesuits,
and their controlling the United States and other countries.

Edited by William Dean A. Garner
New York Times bestselling ghostwriter/editor

The sequel to **Who Really Owns Your Gold**, Third Edition

A critical analysis of the original 36 sermons of Jmmanuel, the man known to the world as **Jesus Christ**

SEAN MACLAREN

ARCANUM

A critical analysis of the original 36 sermons of Jmmanuel,
the man known to the world as Jesus Christ

Available from Amazon.com and other bookstores

eBook available from Amazon.com, AdagioPress.com and
WilliamDeanAGarner.com

In Part 1, Maclaren psychoanalyzes Jmmanuel's sermons, which are featured in Part 2. In Part 3, Maclaren reveals The Laws of Creation that Jmmanuel discussed but never actually revealed in depth.

Edited by William Dean A. Garner
New York Times bestselling ghostwriter/editor

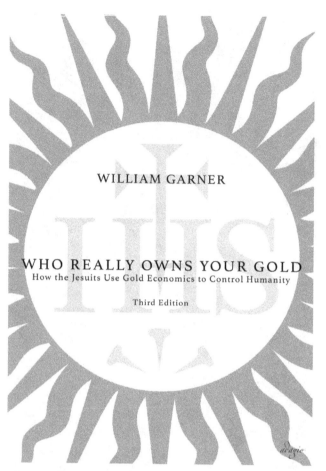

WILLIAM GARNER

WHO REALLY OWNS YOUR GOLD
How the Jesuits Use Gold Economics to Control Humanity

Third Edition

Who Really Owns Your Gold, 3rd Edition

How the Jesuits Use Gold Economics to Control Humanity

Available from Amazon.com and other bookstores

eBook available from Amazon.com, AdagioPress.com and
WilliamDeanAGarner.com

Who Really Owns Your Gold, Third Edition, is about much more than just gold economics. It's about the manipulation of every sector of life across the globe by a dynastic group of men in Rome, the Jesuits, who are successfully building a world that is counter to every good belief we hold dear and true.

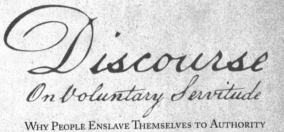

Discourse on Voluntary Servitude
Why People Enslave Themselves to Authority
Available from Amazon.com and other bookstores

Étienne de La Boétie's masterpiece is still highly relevant today. While short in words, it speaks volumes to all those who value liberty on all levels, but who are currently trapped in the yoke of oppression by the many tyrants in every government and institution. This book may be considered the flip-side to Machiavelli's *The Prince*, which teaches would-be dictators how to acquire and maintain power over people and institutions.

ALL-NEW 3RD EDITION

"The best ever DIY book on
filing a veteran's disability claim."
—LawyersAndSettlements.com

VA DISABILITY CLAIM

How to Prepare, File and Maintain a VA Disability Claim and Appeal

JON MACINTOSH

adagio

VA Disability Claim, 3rd Edition

How to Prepare, File and Maintain a VA Disability Claimand Appeal

Available from Amazon.com and other bookstores

eBook available from Amazon.com, AdagioPress.com and
VADisabilityClaimBook.com

VA Disability Claim, Third Edition, has been revamped to reflect the hundreds of suggestions from discerning and caring veterans who commented on the first two editions.

The current book omits the considerably damning intel on VA malpractice and malfeasance, and strictly focuses on how to prepare, file and maintain a VA disability claim and appeal.

How To
1. Sex it like a porn star
2. Write your first book
3. Earn a million bucks
A Simple & Practical Method For
Anyone Who Can Tell A Story

New York Times bestselling ghostwriter & editor
WILLIAM GARNER
adagio

How To Write Your First Book
A Simple and Practical Method for Anyone Who Can Tell a Story
Available from Amazon.com and
other bookstores

eBook available from Amazon.com, AdagioPress.com and
WilliamDeanAGarner.com

This gem is much more than just a book about writing. It reveals metaphysically how our subconscious functions during the creative process to produce the finished product, and how we grow spiritually as this process evolves before us to create our first book.

Garner employs a simple, step-by-step method we have used all our lives, and includes easy-to-follow examples and exercises, plus anecdotes from his work as a ghostwriter/editor.

Rome is in constant conspiracy against the rights and liberties of man all over the world; but she is particularly so in the United States.

—Rev. Charles Chiniquy
in Fifty Years in the Church of Rome

Edited by William Garner
New York Times bestselling Ghostwriter/Editor

ROME'S RESPONSIBILITY
For the Assassination of Abraham Lincoln

How the Jesuits Murdered America's Beloved President

THOMAS M. HARRIS

AN INDEPENDENT PUBLISHING CRUISE
est. January 1, 2001

Katharine L. Petersen
Publisher / Senior Editor
William Dean A. Garner
Editor

Copyright © 2016 Adagio Press

Published in America by Adagio Press

Adagio and colophon are Trademarks of Adagio Press

Library of Congress Control Number: 2016962237

ISBN: 978-1-944855-04-8

Adagio website: AdagioPress.com

Cover design and layout: Dean Garner

B20161214
First Print Edition

for You, dear Reader

Contents

Publisher's Note

Adagio Press is honored to re-release another well-researched and written book about Jesuit machinations in America: *Rome's Responsibility for the Assassination of Abraham Lincoln* by Thomas Harris, originally published in 1897.

General Harris details new facts about the intricate plot by the Jesuits and introduces several new characters who participated in this grand conspiracy to murder an American president on our soil, and further their control of our government and all her people.

The original book has been revamped on all levels, with a new layout and design and cover.

Plus, we have lightly edited the words and grammar of General Harris for clarity.

William Garner
Cape Town, Western Cape
December 2016

Prefatory Note

General Harris needs no word of introduction from me; and yet it may not be amiss to detain the reader just a moment with some allusion to the General's eminent adaptability to do the work which he has so nobly performed in this unpretentious volume.

The author passes his 84th "milestone" today. He has been a painstaking student and careful observer of the teachings and practices of Romanism. He knows his subject fully along the lines of historical Romanism. And being a member of the "Military Commission" that tried and condemned the conspirators, he had unusual opportunities for accurate knowledge concerning Rome's responsibility for the "Crime of the Ages," the assassination of Abraham Lincoln.

And he has here presented a chain of evidence which ought to result in the expulsion of the Jesuits from American soil.

The book deserves to be read and pondered by every American freeman.

I cannot better close this note than in the words of Lincoln himself. In 1864, he said: "If the American people could learn what I know of the fierce hatred of the priests of Rome against our institutions, our schools, our most sacred rights, and our so dearly bought liberties, they would drive them out as traitors."

J. D. Williams
Pittsburgh, PA
June 17, 1897

Dedication

To the memory of our Martyred President, Abraham Lincoln; to all who love the Flag of our country; to all lovers of Liberty and haters of Despotism; to all who are loyal to the Constitution and Government of the United States of America, and who value the rights and the protection which these secure to us: liberty of conscience, freedom of thought and investigation, freedom of speech and the press, within the limitations of the law; the complete separation of Church and State, as distinct and separate organizations, each being independent of the other in its own proper sphere of action, yet not so as to separate religion from the State; civil government being an ordinance of God, and to be administered under His authority, in accordance with the great moral requirements of the Decalogue; to the friends of popular education at the expense of the State; and to all who hope to subserve the highest interests of mankind, and to attain to the true ideal of human existence on earth through the maintenance of these Protestant ideas and institutions, this little book is respectfully and fraternally dedicated by its author.

T. M. Harris
Harrisville, WV

Introduction

This little book is a book of facts. Every statement in it can be sustained by ample testimony.

It reveals a state of things that calls for the earnest and careful consideration of every true American citizen. It shows that we have a most wily and dangerous foe in our midst; that, in fact, we have taken a viper into our bosom, and have, by our genial and hospitable treatment of it, given it sufficient vital vigor to enable it to begin to use its sting.

That foe is the Roman Catholic Hierarchy.

NOTE: It is the governing power of the Roman Catholic Church, the Hierarchy, and not the church in the whole body of the membership that we arraign, and characterize as a foe. There are many of the individual members of the Roman Catholic Church amongst its laity in the United States that really love, and are loyal to our civil institutions.

These, however, are found almost exclusively amongst those who have been educated in our Public Schools; and so have caught the spirit of our institutions and have reached such an appreciation of their God-given rights of manhood as enables them to disregard the assumed authority of their priests over them in civil affairs. These, and these alone, amongst the laity of the Roman Catholic Church, are able to become true and loyal citizens of our Republic.

It is to prevent the multiplication of this class that the Hierarchy of the church uses all its power to keep the children of the church out of our Public Schools. The Parochial school education is directed, and intended, to secure loyalty to the Hierarchy, and to prepare the minds of its children for disloyalty to any other power.

And so it comes to pass that but a comparatively very small moiety of its laity can be depended upon, in any test emergency, for loyalty to our government. But it is only the governing power of the Roman Catholic Church that we arraign. It alone is responsible for the attitude of its laity toward our institutions, and for the control of their conduct; and this Hierarchy is a deadly and implacable foe to our government. The reader of this little book will see that we have ample reasons for making this charge.

This being true, the great body of American freemen should be made to know the fact, and to realize its importance; that they may be prepared to meet, intelligently, the crisis that is upon us. But how shall they be put in possession of a full knowledge of the situation that confronts us? The Hierarchy has attained to such a position of power in this "land of the free" that it is able to control, to a great extent, all of the natural channels of information.

Wherever the Roman Catholic Church is strong, it uses force to suppress freedom of speech, and this evidently at the instigation of the priesthood.

Patriotic lecturers must make up their minds to be courageous enough to encounter the violence of the mob. This experience is, in this free country, and in this enlightened age, a thing of almost daily occurrence. It is the Roman Catholic Church alone that so educates its membership as to have them give this exhibition of their determination to suppress freedom of speech, whenever and wherever they have the power.

In suppressing freedom of the press, the Hierarchy has been

still more successful. By the skillful use of her almost boundless wealth, Rome has secured control of the public press, can put before the American people just what she chooses, and can withhold from them whatever she chooses to suppress.

Thus we find ourselves in such a situation today, that a book like this, cannot hope to be brought to public notice through this channel. Outside of the Patriotic press, there is scarcely a newspaper in the land that would dare to notice this little book, except to misrepresent, and condemn it. There is scarcely a bookseller or news dealer in the United States that would dare to expose it for sale, for fear of that exclusively Roman Catholic weapon, the "boycott."

How, then, shall it find its way to publicity? The information which it contains ought to be in the possession of every voter in the land; and of every American citizen; but how is it to gain the publicity that it ought to have? There is but one channel open to it, and that is found in the various Patriotic organizations that exist throughout the country.

Every member of every one of these various organizations should make it a matter of conscientious duty to interest himself in its circulation.

Every Patriotic lecturer should be prepared to furnish it to any with whom he may come in contact who may desire, or can be prevailed upon to read it. Its price puts it within the reach of all; and it should be circulated by the millions throughout the length and breadth of the land. The suggestions which I have indulged in at its close are intended to be tentative rather than arbitrary.

They, of course, express my own conclusions in regard to what will be found necessary to break, for good and all, the power of the Hierarchy; yet, I do not desire to be dictatorial. I simply invite for them a careful, unbiased, consideration.

It will be for the American people in the exercise of their collective wisdom to determine upon the best course of action. Something must be done, and they will have to determine as to the best method of doing that something.

May God, in His infinite mercy, give us wisdom and courage to do the right and necessary thing, and to face and overcome the foe. As it is only the claim of the Hierarchy of sovereign, civil dominion for its head that we oppose and resist; so, it is only in our civil action, in the discharge of our duties of citizenship, that we can successfully resist this monstrous claim.

It is Rome in politics that we are called upon to fight. With the religion of the Roman Hierarchy we have nothing to do in this field of contention. We accord to every man the right to choose his religion for himself and be answerable only to his God.

1

The Contest Between
Freedom and Despotism

The Anti-Catholic agitation that is now so rife in the United States, marks a crisis in our history. Hundreds of intelligent, patriotic, conscientious men are earnestly, laboriously, and courageously devoting themselves to this agitation.

Newspapers have sprung up all over the country to give warning of danger, and to arouse the spirit of American patriotism.

Societies are being organized all over the land to protect and defend American institutions against the aggressions and encroachments of a Foreign political power that has gotten a lodgement in this land of Liberty, and that is evidently bent on the destruction of our free institutions, and substituting for them the Papal despotism; a despotism that lords it over the minds, the consciences, and the actions of its subjects; and thus renders them incapable of loyalty to any other government.

What does it all mean? It is evident that a crisis is even now upon us; a crisis in which the world-old contest between freedom and despotism is to be definitely and finally settled.

This is an old fight. The cause of liberty seemed to have

achieved the victory when our forefathers achieved their independence through a successful revolution and founded our government on the principles for the first time formally announced in our Declaration of Independence; securing to our people the natural rights of man: freedom of the mind and conscience, freedom of worship, and freedom of speech and of action, and protection in the exercise of these rights.

Here, in the wilds of a newly discovered world, was established a well considered, well understood, and truly democratic government; a government "of the people, by the people, and for the people."

The tree of liberty was here planted in a fertile soil, and a congenial clime, and has become a well-rooted, vigorous and fruitful tree, of goodly stature. Its branches overshadow the land, and its fruit is pleasant to the taste. The question now is, shall it be plucked up by the roots, and burned in the fire?

To this question more than twelve million of American freemen, for themselves, their wives, and their children, and in behalf of humanity, return, in the most emphatic manner the answer: "Never!" and stand ready, if need be, to seal that answer with their blood.

The fruit of the tree of liberty is so sweet to the taste, so refreshing and so invigorating that we are ready to say with Patrick Henry, "Give me liberty, or give me death."

2

The Roman Catholic Church: Friend or Foe of Civil Liberty?

It is because of a conviction that our government is threatened by a wily and formidable foe; that the cause of human liberty is in danger that we are in the midst of this anti-Catholic agitation.

Is all this imaginary, or is there a real danger hanging over us like a cloud? Is the Roman Catholic Church the friend or the foe of liberty? Is it a branch of the Church of Christ, in common with the various Protestant denominations, laboring in common with them, for the establishment of Christ's Kingdom on earth?

If we answer this question in the light of history, in the light of present experience, in the light of the monstrous claims of the Pope, in the light of the spirit by which it is everywhere and always animated, and in the light of its present efforts in our country, and in all lands, we must say that it does not, in any degree, bear the marks of a church of Christ.

It is, in fact, only a compact, well-organized, and powerful political machine, wielded in the interest of the greatest despotism that has ever cursed the earth.

"If any man have not the spirit of Christ, he is none of His;" and if this organization has not the spirit of Christ, it is not a church of Christ.

That it is not animated by the Christ spirit is clearly manifest. It has never manifested the spirit of Christ in all of its past history, and so is not a Christian church at all; and as it has always been grasping after temporal power and civil domination, and is now, as it always has been, laboring for civil supremacy all over the world, we are surely warranted in calling it a huge and dangerous political machine, that has stolen the livery of heaven to enable it the more effectually to serve the Devil; and the more easily to deceive and enslave mankind.

But are our institutions in danger from this foe? Have we any cause for alarm? Is it necessary that we should sound the trumpet throughout the length and breadth of our land, and muster the hosts of freedom for the conflict?

Yes, my fellow countrymen; there is cause for alarm, there is real danger in the immediate situation. "Forewarned, forearmed;" and we have not begun a moment too soon, to organize for the protection of American institutions.

Every citizen, and every sojourner in this country, who is loyal to the Roman Catholic Church, is an enemy to our government, of necessity, for he yields his highest allegiance to the Pope of Rome, a foreign potentate, who has time and again anathematized every fundamental principle of our government. He has denounced liberty of conscience, freedom of speech and of press, freedom of worship and of teaching, as pestilent and damnable heresies; destructive to order, and to the peace and welfare of society.

The highest dignitaries of this so-called church have declared their purpose to make this a Roman Catholic country; but to do this it must be brought to the acceptance of the Pope of Rome as Christ's vicegerent, or representative on earth, invested with all temporal and spiritual authority; above all kings, emperors, and civil rulers; the supreme judge and law-giver, whose decisions are infallible and final.

This would make him lord of the conscience and master of the actions of all men throughout his dominion, which is nothing less than the earth. These are his monstrous claims; and his priests, of all grades, including the wily Jesuits, are laboring night and day to make them good in this land of ours.

Has not the beast of prophecy indeed followed the woman into the wilderness to destroy her child, whose name is Liberty?

It is but a few years since Archbishop Ireland—who poses as a Republican, and as a friend of our government; and who so busied himself in our late Presidential election; and who, since the election, has had the ear of the President, and busies himself in trying to control his most important appointments in the interests of his church—declared that this country was to be brought under the Pope within the next twenty years.

But let things go on for twenty years more as they have been going for the last fifty years, and this will not appear to have been an unwarranted prophecy.

It is evident that Rome is in politics, and is ceaselessly on the alert, in the United States, to so control the political action of our people that whatever party may succeed to power, she may be in the saddle, to augment her wealth and power. And the people are asleep, and must be awakened and made to realize the danger, or our ship of state will be scuttled and sunk.

Is there no danger when the Roman Hierarchy quarters its wily agents in the capital of our nation to exert their influence in shaping our laws, and in controlling Presidential appointments to the highest and most important offices? Is there not danger when all our politicians who aspire to national fame feel that in order to succeed they must truckle to Rome and be submissive? Is there not danger when the capital of our nation has been captured by the wily Jesuit, and Washington is literally "in the lap of Rome?"

Go into any and all of the departments of our government and find seven elevenths of the government employees in several of them, abject slaves of the Pope, and tell me is there no danger?

Go into all our cities and larger towns and find our municipal governments in the hands of the faithful servants of this foreign despot, the Pope, and who are corruptly administering their affairs to enrich the church at the expense of the people, and tell me, is there no danger?

Contemplate this alien and dangerous power in complete control of three-fourths of our newspapers and periodicals, and tell me, is there no danger?

Look at this alien organization levying tribute continually on Protestant business men all over the land, and growing rich on tribute thus levied, and secured through fear of the boycott, and then tell me, if you can, that there is no danger?

Look at the Protestant pulpit, for the most part muzzled and dumb through fear of the boycott against their members who are engaged in business, and on whom they largely depend for their salaries, and then tell me, if you can, that there is no danger.

3

The Advancement of Romish
Control Over the United States

It is clear that Rome is rapidly getting control of all the sources of power in the United States, both in civil and military affairs; that she is doing so in pursuance of a well-considered and wisely laid plan, and for the very purpose of subverting our government.

Let us go back a little and review the means suggested and considered for bringing the United States under the control of the Papacy.

Father Chiniquy, in his book, "Fifty Years in the Church of Rome," gives an extended and minute account of the plans that were discussed by bishops and priests for the attainment of political control of the United States, and for the overthrow of our government.

About fifty years ago, a council of bishops and priests was assembled at Buffalo, N.Y., for the purpose of determining this question.

The Bishop of Chicago thought to accomplish the desired end by colonizing emigrants from Canada, France, and Belgium in such numbers in the valley of the Mississippi, as would give to the Roman Catholic Church political control of the States of Illinois, Indiana, Missouri and Iowa. It was thought that with the fast hold the church had gained in the Southern States, as also in Michigan and Wisconsin, that it would thus be able to hold a cordon of States extending from Florida along the Gulf of Mexico, and up the Mississippi, to our Northern limits, and thus, in time, give it complete political control of the United States.

Father Chiniquy had been engaged in this scheme by the Bishop of Chicago and had entered upon the work as an emigration agent, with enthusiasm, and was meeting with encouraging success. This plan of operations was being advocated earnestly by De Prey Magee, the editor, at that time, of the *Freeman's Journal.*

Promising as it appeared to its advocates, it was repudiated by a large majority of the members of the Buffalo Conference. They argued that by this plan their forces would be scattered, and the power of the church dissipated, and that the true policy of the church for getting political control of the country, was to concentrate its forces in the cities and larger towns, and fill these up, as rapidly as possible, with their foreign emigrants.

It was argued that in this way the Roman Catholic vote could be so wielded, under the direction of the bishops and priests, as to be made a balance of power vote between the two political parties, and so, necessary to the success of either. Being so, it could make its own terms with the political party leaders, and thus get the control of the municipal offices in a very short time; and that it would, in a few years, become a majority vote, when it would have complete control in municipal governments, and ultimately in State politics.

This plan had been carefully thought out and matured by the Jesuits, and its wisdom was made so apparent by their arguments in this conference that the plan of the Bishop of Chicago and his adherents received a very emphatic condemnation by the Buffalo Conference, and the wise plan of the Jesuits was adopted, and at once entered upon, as the true policy of the church for getting political control of our government.

The wisdom of this plan is seen in its results. A half-century has elapsed since its adoption. The work of bringing Roman Catholic emigrants into our country and colonizing them in our cities has been sedulously pursued from that day to this, and the results predicted by the most sanguine of its advocates have been realized.

Quietly, stealthily, steadfastly, has this plan been pursued, under the direction of the most astute political managers that the world has ever seen, until the realization of its purpose seems to be almost within their grasp.

And what was its avowed purpose? Political control of our country was its immediate purpose, but this control was to be used for the overthrow of our government.

The Roman Catholic priesthood, in former years, was wont to protest, loudly, that it took no part in politics, but confined itself to the spiritual interests of mankind; but in all this history of its doings, it is made manifest that the purpose of these gratuitous protestations was to lull us to sleep, to keep hidden from our eyes its evil intent upon our civil and religious liberties.

Having secured the foothold that it has, its attitude is now changed, and it seems desirous to be known as a powerful factor in our political affairs, and to exhibit itself as holding a club over political aspirants; hence it boasts openly made of late, that it has made and unmade Presidents. It still works in secret, and in the dark, but emboldened by its success, it is beginning, upon occasions, to show its hand in the open light of day.

But the eyes of the people are beginning to be opened to the danger, as witness to this present anti-Catholic agitation. There are still greater signs of approaching danger than any that have been above noticed.

What is the rational significance of the fact, that the young men of this so-called church, are being organized into military companies, and regularly drilled in the manual of arms and in tactics? What does it mean that a systematic process of procuring arms and ammunitions is being put into operation? What does it mean that the basements of churches, cathedrals, and school buildings are being converted into arsenals, in which to store away arms and munitions of war?

Does it not indicate a purpose, if need be, in the struggle for supremacy, to resort to revolution and bloodshed?

Is it a mere happen so, that the rank and file in the army of the United States is made up, very largely, of the subjects of this foreign potentate, the Pope of Rome; men, who from their childhood have been taught implicit obedience to his authority as the price of the salvation of their souls, and who, in a conflict of authority between the Pope and the government of the United States, would, without hesitation, yield allegiance to the Pope?

It is not a fact worthy of some thought that a very undue proportion of the field and line officers in our arms are members of this church, and that the same state of things is found in our navy?

Is it not a fact that demands our attention that a largely undue proportion of the cadets in our military schools are members by birth, baptism, and confirmation, of the Roman Catholic Church?

Do not these very significant and important facts clearly indicate that there is an unseen power holding watch and guard over, and controlling these things?

It was this same unseen power that recently secured the promotion of Colonel Coppinger to a Brigadier Generalship, over the heads of about twenty brave officers of American birth, who stood above him on the roster for promotion, and whose military records were as good as his.

Who was this Colonel Coppinger? An Irish adventurer, who commenced his military career in the army of the Pope, where he spent a year in fighting against the freedom of Italy from the grasp of the Papacy. He then came to the United States in the early part of our civil war, and very soon after his arrival at New York, was able to command sufficient influence to get him a commission in the line of a New York regiment.

He served on the side of the Union with such distinction as to win promotions in the volunteer service; and to secure a place on the roster of the regular army, at its reorganization, at the close of the war, where, at the time of this last promotion he held a colonel's commission.

His military record was good; but his personal record was despicable. He was able, however, to secure such influences in his favor as to cause President Cleveland to promote him over about twenty colonels whose military records were as good as his, and whose personal records were unblemished, and whose only fault was that they were Americans and Protestants. His confirmation was opposed actively in the Senate; but the Jesuits triumphed and he was confirmed.

There is a great effort now being made by the Hierarchy to secure a concession from the War Department to build a Roman Catholic Church on the Military reservation at West Point. The purpose of this reservation was the establishment of a National Military School for the education of officers of the army of the United States. It is entirely under the ownership and control of the government; and so knows nothing of sects in religion; but, being a Christian government, it provides a chapel and a chaplain for the use and service of this great National Military School.

But this does not satisfy the ambitious designs of Rome. She seeks to be so far recognized by the government as to be permitted to build a chapel for the exclusive use of the Roman Catholics; and in the contention which has sprung up over this question, it has been stated by the representatives of the Hierarchy, as an argument in favor of the concession which it seeks, that two-thirds of the enlisted men on duty at West Point, and five of the officers there in command, and the family of a sixth, are members of the Roman Catholic Church.

The only use I now intend to make of this reference is simply to ask the question, "How does it come about that Rome has gotten such a hold in our army? Is it a purely accidental thing that five of the officers and two-thirds of the enlisted men on duty at this Military School of the United States Government, are Roman Catholics?"

And why does this so-called church, alone, so anxiously seek this concession? Does it not from all this plainly appear that Rome is laboring to Romanize our army? For what purpose, let us ask ourselves, does she need this military control that she is so anxiously and cunningly seeking and obtaining?

Could we safely commit our institutions to the keeping of a hostile army? Or a soldiery under the control of a despotism that is obviously laying its wires to destroy our civil institutions? In view of Rome's disloyalty, in our late civil war, can we trust her? Is this a Roman Catholic country?

In view of the facts above recited, are there not good

grounds for the conclusion that the wily Jesuits are secretly watching and ceaselessly working to get hold of all the sources of political power in the United States; as also of that which we must ultimately rely for defense of our institutions, our army and navy? Is it not time that the American people should have their attention called to these things, and to their significance?

It is the mission of the Christian church to publish the Gospel of Life and Salvation, through the "blood of the everlasting covenant," to a lost and ruined world; to seek, and to save, the lost; to usher in the era of love, and peace, and joy, throughout the world. Its mission is to be accomplished through the power of the truth, applied to the minds and consciences of men by the Holy Spirit. It has no use for carnal weapons in the prosecution of its work. Its only legitimate weapon is the Word of God, which is "the Sword of the Spirit."

An organization that is always and everywhere grasping after wealth and power—using and preparing to use, carnal weapons, not even hesitating at war and bloodshed—whose aim and effort is to enslave the minds, consciences, bodies and souls of men, fostering the most monstrous and wicked superstitions that it may fill its coffers with gold; that withholds from its members the Word of God, and that puts the decisions and decrees of Popes and church councils in the place of the Scriptures of Divine Truth, as the rule of life, surely cannot be recognized as a Christian church.

No! It is simply a political machine for the enslavement of mankind. It is a monstrous despotism, relying on ignorance, and its natural offspring superstition for its support. It is not a religion that we are called upon to fight, but a corrupt and most dangerous political organization, whose purpose is nothing short of the destruction of our government. Whatever it may be as a religion does not concern our present contention.

Every true American citizen believes in securing to every man freedom of the mind and conscience in the matter of religion, and will ever stand ready to protect him in his right to worship God according to the dictates of his conscience. We do not inquire into the truth or falsity of his religion. We accord to him the right to determine this for himself, and be answerable only to his God.

It is not its religion that we call into question when we arraign the Roman Catholic Church. We only fight it in its political aspirations; and because it is the desperate and deadly foe to civil liberty.

It is, moreover, an active and aggressive foe; a foe that can never be conciliated, never trusted; for when it professes friendship for our institutions, its only purpose is to throw us off of our guard that it may the more surely undermine and destroy them. We know that, should it ever gain political control in our land, it would deprive us of the rights that we now accord it.

It is an organized despotism, and the sworn and implacable foe of liberty. It hates the symbol of the policy, power, and authority of our government, the flag of our country; and places over it the Papal rag. It gives to the highest officer of our government, the president of the United States, the second place at its festal board, reserving the place of honor to the ablegate of the Pope. This insult it has recently perpetrated upon us in the open light of day; and in the most conspicuous and offensive manner—an insult that causes the blood of every American patriot to tingle with resentment.

It is but too evident that no matter what may be its professions, it is, at heart, disloyal to our government; and only loyal to the pope of Rome.

This alien power is the implacable foe of popular education, and is constantly laboring for the destruction of our system of free schools. Her real motive for this opposition lies in the fact that the mental training which her children would get in our free schools, would unfit them for being loyal, obedient and servile children of the church.

Here they would be trained to think, to reason and to investigate; to take nothing on trust, but to form their opinions upon all subjects from convictions resulting from a free and rational investigation. The whole atmosphere of the free school, and all of its associations, would beget in them a love of liberty.

This system of education is the exact counterpart of the system of the parochial schools, and is destructive to that blind faith and servile obedience, that vie to the Roman Catholic Church its power. Our free school system tends to make its beneficiaries good, intelligent, and loyal American citizens, whilst the parochial schools only aim to make their pupils to be loyal subjects of the Papacy. Under the protection of our flag, they are raising up a force to be used for the destruction of our government.

In this contention over the question of education, Rome is continually making efforts to unite the church and the State, by securing the aid of the State in supporting her schools; as also of what she calls her charitable institutions.

By thus attacking the fundamental principles of our government at every point, she makes manifest her disloyalty, and her purpose to undermine and overthrow our institutions. Our civil and religious institutions had their origin in the protest of Luther and his coadjutors against the despotism and corruption of the Roman Catholic Church, that brought about the Reformation of the 16th century. Against this Reformation she has never ceased to fight, and never will, until her power shall have been overthrown.

She has always been the sworn enemy of our Protestant institutions; and is today, as she ever has been, bent on their destruction. She has never lost an opportunity to give them a stab in the dark.

In our dissensions over the questions of slavery, she thought she saw a chance to destroy our government and taking the side of slavery, used her whole influence in the South, to stimulate and encourage secession and rebellion, and in the North to discredit and weaken the cause of the Union.

It was G. T. Beauregard, a rabid Roman Catholic, who first fired on the flag of our country at Fort Sumter; and let loose the dogs of war. It was the Pope of Rome, and he alone, of all the European potentates that gave his recognition and his blessing to the Confederate government; and by the very terms of his kind letter to its president, made it manifest that he expected, through his kind offices, to secure its recognition of his claims, and win it for the church.

It was the Pope of Rome, and his faithful lieutenant, Louis Napoleon, who, taking advantage of our civil war, undertook to establish a Roman Catholic empire in Mexico, and for this purpose sent Maximilian, a Roman Catholic prince, under the protection of a French army, to usurp dominion, and take possession of the country.

All of this was done in the hope that the Union cause would be lost; and that through the strife that she had fomented, two Roman Catholic empires would be established on the American continent, viz. that of Mexico under Maximilian and that of the Confederacy under Jefferson Davis; thus making it possible to make a conquest of the entire continent.

This letter of the Pope to Jefferson Davis, couched in such courteous and loving terms, and showing so clearly that his sympathy was with the Southern cause, was well understood by his loyal and faithful subjects all over the North. Roman Catholic officers began to resign and the rank and file began to desert, from the time of the publication of that letter in 1863 to the close of the war.

In reply to the boast so freely made by Roman Catholic editors and orators that the Irish fought the battles of the civil war and saved the nation, the following document, received from the Pension department at Washington, is here given:

Whole number of troop 2,128,200
Natives of the United States 1,627,267
Germans . . . .
180,817
Irishmen . . . .
144,221
British (other than Irish) 90,040
Other foreigners and missions 87,855
The "Desertions" were as follows:
Natives of the United States 5
percent
Germans . . . . 10 percent
Irish Catholics . . . . 72 percent
British (Other than Irish) . . . . 7 percent
Other foreigners . . . . 7 percent

In other words; of the 144,000 Irishmen that enlisted, 104,000 deserted.

And it is reliably stated that most of these desertions occurred after the recognition of the Confederacy by the Pope. It is also a fact that of the five percent of native Americans rated as deserters, 45 percent of the 5 percent were Catholics.*

This is a sufficient proof of the charge heretofore made that a good Roman Catholic can only be loyal to the Pope and so can never be loyal to our government, and to our Protestant institutions.

It is true that there were some able and brave Roman Catholic officers in the Union army, who were truly loyal to the cause; as also many in the ranks who were nominally members of the Roman Catholic Church; but these were they who had been educated in our free schools, and had thus become so imbued with the American Spirit, that they were no longer good Catholics. All honor to these!

Not only by desertions and resignations was Roman Catholic disloyalty made apparent, but more conspicuously by the draft riots that followed—the rioters being made up, almost entirely, of Irish Roman Catholics.

Archbishop Hughes posed as a Union man; and was so far trusted by President Lincoln, that he solicited his good offices at Rome, to prevent the Pope from giving recognition to the Confederate government; he being well aware of the consequences that would follow such recognition. The Archbishop proved a traitor to his trust; and the Pope's letter to Jefferson Davis followed closely on the heels of his visit to Rome, and resignations and desertions commenced.

Then followed the terrible riots in New York City, when a draft became necessary to fill up our depleted ranks. For three fearful days and nights the city was terrorized by the violence of an Irish Catholic mob, right under the shadow of the Archbishop's palace.

The Archbishop kept secluded in his palace, and as mute as a mouse, until notified by Mr. Lincoln that he would be held personally responsible for its continuance. He then came forth; and by a few kind words to the rioters, whom he addressed as his friends, the mob immediately dispersed, and order was restored. It only took a few words from him to accomplish what could not have been accomplished without much bloodshed, and perhaps the destruction of the city, by a military arm of our government; but mark those words were not spoken until it became necessary to the personal safety of the Archbishop. The traitor was here revealed.

And now we come to the last desperate conspiracy to overthrow our government, and make the rebellion a success by a resort to the favorite policy of the Jesuits, that of assassination.

It is my purpose now to review the facts connected with the assassination of President Lincoln, and the attempted assassination of Mr. Seward, and the purpose to assassinate Vice-president Johnson, Secretary Stanton and General Grant. The object of this scheme of wholesale assassinations of the civil and military heads of the government, was to throw the country into a state of chaos, and thus retrieve the fast failing fortunes of the Confederacy.

These facts, as developed on the trial of the conspirators before a military commission, and on the trial of John H. Surratt two years later, before a civil court, together with evidence secured by Father Chiniquy, and given to the world in his book, "Fifty Years In The Church Of Rome," show conclusively the hand of Rome in this stab at our nation's life.

I will now proceed to pass these facts in review, in their proper order, and to show their significance.**

I do not propose to affirm or deny the charge that is now being commonly and openly made by patriotic papers and lecturers that Rome was responsible for the assassination of our martyred President, but simply to present the facts, and leave my readers to draw their conclusion from a consideration of the facts in the case.

My own personal convictions will no doubt be made obvious

before I get through. The very fact that the charge is being made by a high class of men—men noted for intelligence, patriotism and uprightness of character—justifies us in making a careful scrutiny of the evidence on which it rests; that we may fairly judge whether or not it has been justly made. It is a charge of too much gravity and of too serious an import to be made lightly, or on insufficient grounds.

---

* Toledo American, as quoted on page 115 of "Why I am an A.P.A."
** For a full account of which, see my book entitled, "Assassination of Lincoln, A History of the Great Conspiracy and Trial of the Conspirators by a Military Commission and a Review of the Trial of John H. Surratt."

4

Facts Regarding the Execution
of the Plot to Assassinate
Abraham Lincoln

Now for the facts. And we will take, as our starting point, the fact well established: that the headquarters of the conspiracy in Washington City was the house of a Roman Catholic family, of which Mrs. Mary E. Surratt was the head; and all of its inmates, including a number of boarders, were devoted members of the Roman Catholic Church.

This house was the meeting place, the council chamber, of Booth and his co-conspirators, including Mrs. Mary E. Surratt, and her son, John H. Surratt, who, next to Booth, were the most active members of the conspiracy in preparation for the execution of the plot.

Booth, the ringleader, was born and reared a Protestant. He was only a nominal Protestant, however. He was man of the world; a drunkard and a libertine, and utterly indifferent to matters of religion.

That under the influence of his associations in the conspiracy plot—he had become a pervert to Catholicism—was shown, however, by the fact that, on examination of his person after his death, it was found that he was wearing a Catholic medal under his vest, and over his heart.

The wily Jesuit, sympathizing with him in his political views, and in hope of destroying our government, and establishing the Confederacy, which had already received the Pope's recognition, and expressions of good will and sympathy conferred upon it, had been able to pervert him to Catholicism, and to deceive him into the belief that his medal would conduce to his personal safety, and to the success of his enterprise. He had, no doubt, been baptized into the Catholic Church. This medal at once marked and identified him as a pervert to Catholicism.

Now we have Mary E. Surratt, John H. Surratt, J. Wilkes Booth, Dr. Samuel Mudd, and Michael O'Laughlen, five of the leading active spirits in the execution of the plot to assassinate, belonging to the Roman Catholic Church.

My impression is that Herold and Spangler were also members or adherents to that church. Be this as it may, they, together with Atzerodt and Payne, were the mere tools, and hired agents of Booth and Surratt, and so stood ready to serve their purpose; and so it boots not to inquire into their faith or want of faith.

Our inquiry then, thus far, has established the fact that five of the conspirators were members of the Roman Catholic Church and that these five were its leaders, to whom the execution of the plot had been confided.

We have also seen that their meeting place, or council chamber, in Washington, whilst engaged in perfection their arrangements for the assassinations that had been determined upon, was the dwelling place and under the control of Mrs. Mary E. Surratt and John H. Surratt, her son; both of whom were zealous slaves of the Pope, and clearly proven, by the evidence given before the Commission and by that given two years later, on the trial of John H. Surratt in a civil court, to have been leading and active members of the conspiracy.

Mrs. Surratt was a diligent and faithful attendant upon church services; and from the evidence given by three or four priests in her behalf before the Commission, she had established, in their estimation, a high character for devotion and Christian piety.

It was a noteworthy fact, however, that, of all these priestly witnesses, but one admitted that he had been on specially intimate terms with her during the five months in which the plans and preparations for the assassinations were being made. Most of them had been acquainted with her for many years, and seemed to be well acquainted with her church reputation, but they had only seen her casually during these latter months.

One of these, Father Wiget, was Mrs. Surratt's pastor during all this time, and testified that he knew her well; but did not know whether she was loyal or disloyal.

This would seem to be very doubtful testimony, as Father Wiget was noted for his disloyalty, and could hardly have been supposed to have spent many hours with her, at different times, without ever having heard her express her views in relation to the one all-absorbing topic of the time, that was uppermost in the minds of all, and formed the chief topic of conversation.

He could only say that he did not remember having heard her utter a loyal sentiment since the beginning of the rebellion; nor could he remember having heard any one speak of her as notoriously disloyal, until since her arrest. He said he had become acquainted with her through having had the care of two of her sons as his pupils. One of these was serving in the rebel army; and the other, John H. Surratt, had been a rebel emissary and spy for three years, passing back and forth between Washington and Richmond, and from Richmond to Canada and back, as a bearer of dispatches. And yet, this Jesuitical priest, endeavored so to shape his testimony as to leave the impression that the topics of conversation between himself and Mrs. Surratt, whilst all this was going on, and much more, was confined to such topics as the state of her health, the weather, etc. He was very positive as to her good Christian character, which he had been summoned to prove, but had very little recollection of anything else.

Father Boyle, resident at St. Peter's Church, Washington City, had made the acquaintance of Mrs. Surratt eight or nine years previously, but had only met her three or four times since. He had always heard her well spoken of; never had heard anything to her disadvantage; had never heard her utter any disloyal sentiments.

Father Stonestreet, pastor of St. Aloysius Church, Washington City, had made her acquaintance twenty years before; had only occasionally seen her since; had scarcely seen her at all during the last year or two; had always looked upon her a proper Christian matron.

At the time of his acquaintance with her, (which he was locating twenty years back) there was no question of her loyalty. Replying to a question by the Judge Advocate: "He did not remember having seen her, though he might have done so transiently, since the commencement of the rebellion; and knew nothing of her character for loyalty, only what he had seen in the papers."

Father Lanihan, a Catholic priest living near Beantown, in Maryland, testified that he had been acquainted with Mrs. Surratt for about thirteen years; intimately for about nine years; that he had been very familiar with her, staying at her house. He regarded her as a good Christian woman, highly honorable; he had frequently talked with her about current events, and public affairs since the rebellion, but could not remember ever having heard her express any disloyal sentiments; neither had he heard her reputation for loyalty spoken of.

Finally; Father Young, of St. Dominic's Church, on Sixth Street, Washington City, was called in her behalf. He had been acquainted with Mrs. Surratt about eight or ten years, but not intimately; he had occasionally seen her, and visited her; passed her house about once a month, and generally called there, staying sometimes an hour.

He, like the others, was a good witness for her as to her character, but could say nothing as to her loyalty, or disloyalty; he had never heard her speak as to current events one way or another.

How can we credit the testimony of this witness? Is it credible that he could have spent an hour in conversation with a rebel woman of such positive character and convictions, once a month, during the heat of the conflict, and yet never have heard any expressions from her on the subject that filled the minds and hearts of all, and formed the chief topic of conversation, in all classes of society?

Such silence between a rebel woman and a rebel priest, who were on intimate and confidential terms, is too incredible to be believed. We cannot help thinking that all of these holy or unholy Fathers testified under the well understood mental reservations of the Jesuits.

Father Wiget was, as we have said, her pastor, and so, we take it, was her confessor. We cannot think it at all probable that she would have engaged in a conspiracy fraught with so much danger to her, and such grave consequences hereafter, without having confided to him her terrible secret; nor without his approval. It certainly is rather strange that she should have broken her relations with him after her conviction, and taken Father Walter for her confessor and spiritual guide in her preparation for death.

There must have been some grave reason for this change; and it was made for her, by these Jesuit priests, for some important reason. It is not at all likely that at such a time, and under such solemn circumstances, she would have made this change from her pastor to another priest with whom she had not had any previous acquaintance, of her own volition.

Had she been innocent, her trusted pastor would have been the one to whom she naturally would have looked for consolation. But Wiget had no doubt told her that she would incur no guilt in aiding the conspiracy, and so to Walter she could declare her innocence, having the faith of a Catholic in Wiget's power to grant her dispensation.

Father Walter could say "that whilst his priestly vows would not allow him to reveal the secrets of the confessional, he could say, that from what there came to his knowledge, he knew her to be an innocent woman."

There was to be a great effort made to get a commutation, or reversal of her sentence; and the strong plea of the Father was to be based on this assertion of her innocence. Failing in this, Father Walter, for thirty years, persisted in his efforts to fix upon the government the stigma of having murdered an innocent woman.

In its uniting with Father Walter in his effort to fix upon our government the stigma of a great crime, to its eternal disgrace, the Roman Catholic Hierarchy assumed, with him, the responsibility of perverting the well established truths of history, and of thus manifesting their hatred of our government, and their chagrin and bitter disappointment at the failure of their efforts for its overthrow.

So deep, and bitter, was their disappointment at the signal success of the government in the vindication of its authority, and its right to exist, that for a quarter of a century it never ceased its efforts to fix upon it the stigma of this alleged crime, and it was only estopped from this effort by the publication of my "History of the Great Conspiracy" to overthrow our government by a series of assassinations, when, fearing that its further agitation might tend to give publicity to my book, and that thus the facts of this conspiracy would become more widely known, and the truth of history vindicated, that the agitation of this charge, and contention against the government was dropped as it had become a hot potato.

We must not forget, that in all this, they acted under a full knowledge of all the facts in the case. These had been fully displayed to the world through the evidence produced by the government on the trial of the assassins in 1865, and two years later, still more fully, on the trial of John H. Surratt in a civil court. These things were not done in a corner, but openly before the world.

Their sympathy with the conspirators and assassins, and their enmity toward the government, was thus openly proclaimed before the world; and the attitude of the Hierarchy toward the assassination of the nation's head, was clearly manifest. It was Abraham Lincoln, it is true, that was slain, but it was the life of the nation that the blow was aimed at.

The scheme to aid the rebellion by the assassination of the President, the Vice-President, the Secretary of State, the Secretary of War, and the General in command of our armies, was concocted by the emissaries of the rebel government, who kept their headquarters in Montreal, Canada. These emissaries held a semi-official relation to the Confederate government.

The whole run of the evidence makes it clear that the Roman

Hierarchy kept itself in close relations with these emissaries; and it is highly probable, from a consideration of all of the facts, with the head of the government in whose service they were employed also. It kept itself in these close relations for a purpose, and was most likely the original source of the inspiration of the assassination plot.

These rebel emissaries were Jacob Thompson, of Mississippi; Clement C. Clay, of Alabama; and Beverly Tucker of Virginia. These had associated with them as helpers: George N. Sanders, Dr. Blackburn, and others; men who preferred to fight in the field of political strategy, rather than on the field of battle.

These agents of the rebel government entered into a contract with J. Wilkes Booth and John H. Surratt to carry out their scheme, and also aided them in the selection of their subordinates. Whether these emissaries were Protestants or Catholics, I am not informed. My impression, however, is that they were nominally Protestants.

They were all, however, wicked men, evidently accepting the maxim that "all is fair in war," and having no conscientious scruples as to the means that they employed to give aid to their cause.

That the Jesuit had their ear, and aided them with his suggestions, is made probable by the fact, that in his efforts to enlist, as a helper to Booth and Surratt, a young man who was sent before the commission as a witness, on the trial, Thompson used the Jesuitical argument, that to kill a tyrant was no murder; and so, assuming that President Lincoln was a tyrant, it would be a glorious and praiseworthy act to take him off.

5

Assassination Plot Known to the Bishop of Montreal and Other Priests

That the assassination plot was known to the Bishop of Montreal (Bourget) and a number of his priests, before its accomplishment, and received their sanction, was made plain by their subsequent conduct.

As soon as the news of the assassination of the President was flashed over the wires, Fathers Boucher and La Pierre kept themselves on the lookout, and ready to aid any of the conspirators who might make good their escape to Canada.

John H. Surratt and a companion, whose identity was never discovered, returned to Montreal, on the early afternoon of the 18th of April, the fourth day after the assassination. The unknown conspirator then sank out of sight.

Surratt was spirited away from the hotel within fifteen minutes after he had registered on his return. He had registered on the same book, on his return from Richmond to Canada, on the 6th of April, had gone back to Washington and played his part in the conspiracy on the night of the 14th of April, and now, on the afternoon of the 18th had gotten back to Montreal. He was so carefully watched for, that almost at the instant of his arrival, he was spirited away, and kept hidden carefully, in the house of Porterfield; one of Thompson's assistants, who, for his greater security, had relinquished his American citizenship, and had taken the oath of allegiance to the British crown. Porterfield told him that the detectives were on the alert, and lost no time in hiding him away.

Porterfield, deeply exercised for the safety of his charge, as also for his own, only kept him until he could communicate with Father Boucher, a Roman Catholic priest, who lived in an out of the way country parish, forty-five miles from Montreal. Father Boucher immediately sent his servant man to bring Surratt to his place for further hiding.

Du Tilly, Father Boucher's man, arrived before the house of Porterfield late in the evening of the 21st of April, and, taking Surratt into his carriage, drove him away under the cover of darkness, and placed him in the keeping of his master, Father Boucher. Here he remained for two months, under the most careful watch and guard of his keeper. Whilst here, he was visited frequently by some of his friends in whose employ he had incurred his guilt; and by another Father, La Pierre. This La Pierre was canon to Bishop Bourget; ate at his table, and was to him the same as a hand and arm.

A circumstance having occurred that made it necessary for Father Boucher to unload his charge, he sent him back to Montreal, as secretly as he had taken him away from there, and placed him in the care of Father La Pierre.

This Father provided Surratt with an upstairs chamber in his own father's house, right under the shadow of the Bishop's palace. Here he kept him for three months, never permitting him to leave his room in the daytime, and never at night but in company with himself, and in disguise.

Thus was Surratt kept hidden away for five months, in the

care and at the charge of the Roman Catholic Church; two of its priests keeping watch and ward over him, with a full knowledge of his crime, thus making themselves accomplices after the fact, as they also, no doubt were, before its accomplishment.

But how about Bishop Bourget? He stands behind the scenes, it is true, but was he not equally guilty?

The organization of the Hierarchy is a complete military despotism, of which the Pope is the ostensible head; but of which the Black Pope is the real head. The Black Pope is the head of the order of the Jesuits, and is called a General. He not only has the absolute command of his own order, but directs and controls the general policy of the church. He is the power behind the throne, and is the real potential head of the Hierarchy.

The whole machine is under the strictest rules of military discipline. The whole thought and will of this machine, to plan, propose and execute, is found in its head.

There is no independence of thought, or of action, in its subordinate parts. Implicit and unquestioning obedience to the orders of superiors in authority, is the sworn duty of the priesthood of every grade; just as it is the duty of officers in the army, and as much the duty of the laity to their priests, as it is of the rank and file in an army to their immediate commanders. There is a complete chain of responsibility, extending from the head all the way down to the membership.

Thus the whole vast organization can be wielded, as a unit, to accomplish the plans and purposes of its head. The priest is virtually an intellectual slave to his bishop, the bishop to his archbishop, and these again to the cardinals, and all, finally, to the Popes, white and black.

This being the case, it is clear that no priest would have dared to take on himself such grave responsibilities as did

Fathers Boucher and La Pierre, involving so much danger to themselves, as also to the character of their church, without the knowledge and assent of their bishop. It would have been held to be an act of insubordination, fraught with the most serious consequences to themselves.

But the canon occupies a peculiar relation to his bishop, and is supposed to have no other duty, but to carry out the orders which he receives from his superior.

In this view of the case, which represents truly the relations between Bishop Bourget and his Canon, La Pierre, can we rationally come to any other conclusion than that Bourget was in a moral point of view, also a member of the conspiracy; neither would Bishop Bourget have dared to give his consent to this crime on his own independent responsibility. He knew he was acting in harmony with the desire and purpose of the Hierarchy, for the destruction of our government.

The Jesuit plans with the utmost art and cunning, unhampered by any moral restraints, and always with the utmost secrecy; and carries out his plans in the dark. We think, however, that this case, we have succeeded in tracing him through all the devious wanderings of his dark and slimy path, and, in fixing upon him the responsibility for the assassination of President Lincoln.

But we are not done yet. In the early part of September, 1865, these unholy Fathers thought it safe to unload their charge onto their brethren in England; and so made arrangements for sending Surratt across the Atlantic, under an assumed name, and in disguise. For this purpose they arranged for his passage on a British steamer, the Peruvian, which was to sail from Quebec on the 16th of September, 1865.

A physician with whom Boucher was well acquainted, by the name of McMillan, had just gotten the position of surgeon to this vessel, and they arranged with him to take under his especial charge, a man by the name of McCarthy, who, for certain reasons, wished to cross the Atlantic under an assumed name, and in the most secret manner.

The day before the Peruvian was to sail from Quebec, these two unholy Fathers conveyed Surratt, in a covered carriage, to the steamer that was to carry passengers for the Peruvian from Montreal to Quebec. They had disguised Surratt by coloring his hair, painting his face, and putting spectacles over his eyes. Father La Pierre went also in the disguise of a citizen's dress.

Arriving on board the steamer, Surratt was immediately stored away in a stateroom, from which he did not emerge during the voyage, La Pierre remaining in his room with him. Reaching Quebec, these two unholy Fathers placed their charge in the care of Dr. McMillan; and then took their final leave of him.

They had consigned him to the care of their friends in Liverpool, by the hands of Dr. McMillan, and through whose aid Surratt succeeded in placing himself under the care of the Roman Catholic Church in a foreign land.

Rome is everywhere, and always the same, and he can feel safe as long as he is in the custody of the church.

Here he waited for the Peruvian to make another voyage to Quebec and return. He sent by the surgeon, to his rebel employers in Canada, a request to send him some money; but only to receive the answer that they had no money for him. The expense of sending him across the continent, to Italy, thus fell on the church. His rebel friends had now forsaken him; but the church stood by him.

He was sent to Italy and was mustered into the army of the Pope. Here he remained safely hidden away for a year or more; but was finally discovered by a government detective who had been sent in search of him, and who went voluntarily, hoping to get the offered reward, and who had enlisted in the same company to which Surratt belonged.

This detective informed our government of his discovery; and through the agents of our government the Pope was informed that his soldier, who had enlisted under the name of Watson, was none other than the notorious John H. Surratt, who was a member of the conspiracy that accomplished the assassination of President Lincoln.

With a shrewd show of virtuous innocence, the Pope hastened to clear his skirts, and those of his underlings, by ordering his arrest, and rendition to our government, without waiting for its requisition.

He was arrested by the Pope's authority, but was allowed to escape by his guards; and thus given another chance for life and liberty. The story was, that he made his escape by a bold leap over a precipice, at the risk of his life. "Tell this to the marines; the old sailors will not believe it."

He was finally captured at Alexandria, Egypt, and was brought home in chains, where he was held to answer for his crime.

6

The Cunning Hand of the Romish Hierarchy in the Trial of John H. Surratt

Let us here pause a moment to consider the relations of the Hierarchy to this crime.

The testimony given on the trial of John H. Surratt, clearly convicts two of its priests, Boucher and La Pierre, of being accomplices in the conspiracy; and by implication, as clearly convicts the Bishop of Montreal, Bishop Bourget.

This testimony was spread before the world, and so must have been known to the Roman Catholic Hierarchy, yet it never called any of these priests to accountability, or held them responsible for this crime; the crime of the ages! No one of them was ever held to have forfeited his standing or good character in the church, on account of his connection with this conspiracy; and so, the Hierarchy stands before the world today, as having given its approval to their conduct in this matter.

We now come to the trial of John H. Surratt before a civil court. It is not our purpose to go into a general review of the trial, but only to show the interest taken in it by the Roman Catholic priesthood, the animus of the defense toward the government, and the means resorted to, to make sure of his acquittal.

The hand of the Jesuit is everywhere traceable throughout the history of this trial; and by that hand, one of the most important trials that the history of American jurisprudence records, was well nigh turned into a farce by the skill and cunning of the defense.

The cunning of the Jesuit was exercised in the preparations made in advance, to make sure of acquittal of the accused. The law of Congress—specifying particularly how juries to try cases in the criminal court, in the District of Columbia, should be secured—was entirely ignored, in some of its most important and essential particulars.

Counsel for the defense had been selected with special care. There were three of these: Mr. Merrick and the two Bradleys, Sr. and Jr. Of these, only one, Mr. Merrick, was a member of the Roman Catholic Church. The Bradleys were Episcopalians; but in their political sympathies, hostile to the government; and in full sympathy with its enemies, and with the assassins.

When the jury that had been drawn for this trial was challenged by the prosecution, and good reasons shown for its rejection, the counsel for the defense made a most vigorous, earnest and persistent effort to prevent its being set aside by the court.

It is evident that they must have had a special reason for being so urgent for its retention, as the failure of the officers—whose duty it was to secure this jury, to observe the requirements of the law—was made so apparent that it could not be controverted.

It leaked out, however, that sixteen out of the twenty-four drawn were Roman Catholics, and so, the reason for their determined effort for its retention was made obvious. It was set aside, and a venire was summoned, from which to obtain a jury.

A jury was finally obtained, through a two-day effort and, as the prosecution desired to remove, as far as possible, all religious and political considerations and influences from the trial, a considerable number of Roman Catholics were accepted on this jury. The trial then proceeded.

The defense proceeded at once to put the government and not the prisoner at the bar, on trial. They arraigned it for the murder of an innocent woman, Mrs. Surratt; and for having secured her conviction through an illegal tribunal, organized to convict, and not to try. By every means in their power they aroused a partisan spirit of political and religious bigotry; and so, surrounded the court with the air and spirit of a political convention, and removed, as far as possible, from the trial, the air and spirit of a judicial procedure.

The result was a hung jury. The author was informed by a very intelligent man, who took a prominent part in this trial, that, meeting one of the jurors, who appeared to be a very frank and intelligent man, on the day after the trial, he asked him if he felt free to tell how the jury stood. He replied that they were very nearly equally divided for conviction and acquittal.

He then asked him if they did not think that he was proven guilty. "Oh, yes," he replied, "we thought he was proven guilty, but we thought his conviction would be a triumph for the Radicals, and we thought that the hanging of his mother was about enough."

A most noteworthy fact in connection with this trial, as bearing upon the subject of our investigation, was the deep interest manifested by the Roman Catholic priesthood of Washington in this trial; and their sympathy with the accused. There was scarcely a day, during the trial, but what one or more of them was found in the courtroom. They also made it manifest that they were there on behalf of the prisoner at the bar; and that they were ready to aid in his defense was very apparent.

Whenever the prosecution brought a witness on the stand whose testimony was particularly damaging to the accused, a witness was always found to rebut his testimony; and was always a member of the Roman Catholic Church.

It was also a very significant fact, that no one of all these witnesses was able to pass the ordeal of Judge Pierrepont's cross-examination unscathed.

It looked as though the task of these priests was to aid the prisoner's counsel, by finding the witnesses that they needed; and stuffing them with the needed testimony. It was thus made manifest, during the trial, on more than one occasion, that witnesses had been hunted up and furnished with a cooked up testimony to meet the requirements of the case.

It is worthy of note that whenever the prosecution thought it important to rebut any testimony, a witness was always promptly found for them; and was always a Catholic. The manner of these witnesses in testifying and the fact that they could never stand the test of Judge Pierrepont's searching cross-examination, justly gave rise to the suspicion that they had been suborned and were delivering a cooked up testimony. And these facts gave rise to the suspicion that it was the special business of someone to find and stuff the witnesses for the occasion.

John H. Surratt had been a student at St. Mary's College for a year or two, at the breaking out of the war. He had commenced a collegiate course, having the priesthood in view. His sympathies were so strongly with the South that he left the college, gave up his priestly aspirations, and engaged actively in the secret service of the Confederate government.

As a student, he was very popular at the college and seemed

to have won the favor of the president and faculty. The summer vacation at the college occurred during the progress of the trial, and the president took occasion to spend a day in the courtroom, and sat, all day, at the side of the prisoner in the dock.

His presence there was no doubt intended to have its effect on the Roman Catholic members of the jury. It was as much as to say, "You see which side I am on." Many of the students of that college took occasion to visit their former fellow student during the trial; and always manifested their sympathy for him by the warmest friendly greetings; taking their places at his side.

How different was their treatment of his, and their fellow student, L. J. Wiechmann, who has also had the priesthood in view, but finding himself unable to continue at college, turned aside, temporarily, to replenish his pecuniary resources. He first found employment as a teacher in one of the Roman Catholic schools in the city of Washington; but finding a more lucrative position in one of the government offices, in the military department, he resigned his position as teacher, and became a clerk under General Hoffman, who was Commissary General of prisoners.

Mrs. Surratt rented her property at Surrattsville, and took a house in Washington, and as a means of support, took in boarders. Through his acquaintance with her son, John H. Surratt, at St. Mary's College, Wiechmann became an inmate of her house; and boarded and lodged there for some months before, and up to the time of assassination.

In this way he saw many things that occurred in that house in connection with the conspiracy, but without understanding their import; and as he was a very agreeable and obliging young man, bright and intelligent, he seems to have been a favorite with Mrs. Surratt. He frequently escorted her to church, as she was a very devout Catholic; and was used by her on two occasions, just before the assassination, to drive her down to her former home at Surrattsville. The last time was on the afternoon before the assassination.

As soon as the assassination was made known, the military police of the city and General Baker's whole secret service force, were set at work to discover the perpetrators of the crime.

It was soon ascertained that it was John Wilkes Booth who had shot the President; and the detectives soon discovered that Surratt was an accomplice of Booth; and that Booth had been a frequent caller, of late, at the house of Mrs. Surratt. And so, within six hours after the assassination, Mrs. Surratt's house was visited by the detectives, and all of its inmates were kept under their surveillance.

Wiechmann went voluntarily to the Provost Marshall's office—along with another of the inmates of Mrs. Surratt's house, by the name of Holohan—where he submitted honestly and conscientiously, in answer to the questions put to him, and narrated all that he knew in connection with Booth's visits to Mrs. Surratt's house.

This examination developed the fact that Booth's business there was always with John H. Surratt, and in his absence, with his mother; and that it was always strictly private and confidential in its character.

Wiechmann was thus discovered to be an important witness in the case, and was so held by the government.

After the arrest of Mrs. Surratt and Payne, Wiechmann recognized Payne as a man who had made two visits to Mrs. Surratt's; once under an assumed name and other suspicious circumstances, and remaining there three days on the occasion of his last visit. He left for Baltimore, but returned a few days later, clandestinely, to the city, and occupied quarters that had been provided for him by Surratt, where he was kept hidden away; but had been visited, on one occasion, by Mrs. Surratt, to the knowledge of Wiechmann. All of these things he faithfully related to the examining officer.

On the trial of Mrs. Surratt he showed himself to be a conscientious witness to the truth. He was placed in a very delicate and trying position, in being called upon to testify in a case where those with whom he had been intimately associated, and trusted as friends, were on trial for the highest crime that they could have committed; and that involved their lives.

His bearing before the court made it manifest that he felt very deeply the delicacy and gravity of his position; but that he could not shrink from a frank disclosure of the facts that had come within his knowledge, in connection with the case.

The facts disclosed by this witness, taken by themselves, though calculated to give rise to strong suspicions of Mrs. Surratt's connection with the crime, were not sufficient to have convicted her. It was only when the testimony of Lloyd and of Colonel Smith was made to supplement that of Wiechmann, that her guilt was clearly shown.

Because Wiechmann had been thus brought into the case as a witness, and had given an honest and truthful testimony, he was most cruelly followed up with the persecutions of the Roman Catholic priesthood; and was treated, by both priest and layman, as an excommunicated person, only worthy of scorn and contempt; and on no account to be associated with.

He was given to know that he would never be allowed to enter the priesthood; and it was only through the good offices of the government that he was allowed to find any employment by which to gain a livelihood.

He never met the fact of any priest after that, for many years at least, but to see the deepest expression of hatred and scorn. He was completely boycotted, and ostracized by his church.

He was made a witness again on the trial of John H. Surratt, when every effort was made by the counsel for the defense to cause him to contradict the testimony he had given before the commission; but without avail. To discredit him, much of the cooked up testimony previously referred to was brought in.

In this effort, also, they were foiled. He was badgered on the witness stand for two whole days, and treated with the most scornful contempt by the counsel for the defense. He was branded by them as a perjured witness, although they had been unable to impeach him by the methods known to the law.

He was even charged with having been a member of the conspiracy; and that he had testified falsely, to save his own neck by convicting Mrs. Surratt. It was even charged that he had bought his immunity from the government by consenting to give the testimony which it had prepared for him, in order to convict Mrs. Surratt. This charge had also been reiterated publicly, within a very recent period.

Wiechmann was on the witness stand, at the time of the visit of the president of St. Mary's college, and of its students to Surratt, in the courtroom, but could not gain the slightest token of recognition from any of them. They were fast and free to show their warmest sympathy with the man who stood before the world as guilty of the murder of the President of the United States, but would not recognize the man, who, but recently, had stood on equal terms with him at the college, as a fellow student.

And why was this? The only obvious reason was that he had been an honest and conscientious witness to the truth.

The same treatment was given by the counsel for the accused to another witness: Dr. McMillan.

It will be remembered that this witness was the surgeon of the Peruvian, and that it was to his care that Surratt had been committed, under the name of McCarthy, by his co-conspirators, Boucher and La Pierre.

The voyage across the Atlantic occupied seven or eight days, and as the doctor was the only man on board in whom Surratt could confide, and as he was carrying in his breast the secrets of a great crime, that was weighing heavily on his conscience, and being all the time haunted by the spectra of detectives, it was natural that he should seek relief in the confidential companionship of McMillan.

He became very communicative, and related the difficulties that he experienced and overcame, in making good his escape from Washington, and in getting back to Canada, after the assassination—the parts taken by Porterfield, Boucher and La Pierre, in keeping him hidden away in Canada for five months, and many other things relating to the conspiracy; and finally, he revealed to him his identity.

The testimony of this witness was entirely conclusive as to his guilt, and so, he was particularly obnoxious to the prisoner's counsel.

He was treated by them, from the start, just as they would have treated a witness who had been convicted of perjury, although they were unable to discredit him, by the legal methods. They could not look at him, or speak of him, but with the air and language of scorn and contempt.

So important did it seem to discredit this witness, that priest Boucher voluntarily came all the way from Canada, to rebut his testimony. His man, Du Tilly, was also brought; but notwithstanding the fact that they showed themselves to be swift witnesses, of the most ready kind, they failed to discredit this witness.

Under the searching cross-examination of Judge Pierrepont they were made to corroborate the testimony given by the doctor, in all of its most essential and important particulars, and the unholy Father was made to convict himself of being equally guilty with the prisoner.*

*See report of the trial of John H. Surratt, published in two volumes by the government.

7

Testimonial of Rev. Chiniquy

It would seem that the Jesuits had had it in mind, from the beginning of the war, to find an occasion for the taking off of Mr. Lincoln.

Early in the war, they set a paragraph going the rounds of the press, as far as they had it under their control, to the effect that Mr. Lincoln had been born in the Catholic Church, and had been made a member of the church by his baptism into it and that he had apostatized and become a heretic.

Mr. Lincoln had seen this statement going the rounds of the press, and believed that such a gross falsehood would not have been published without a purpose.

On the occasion of a visit from Father Chiniquy about this time, Mr. Lincoln called his attention to this paragraph, saying he had been greatly perplexed in trying to discover the object of its publication; and asking him if he could give any clue to the motive that had inspired such a falsehood.

I will give Father Chiniquy's own account of his interview with the President on this subject:

"The next day, I was there at the appointed hour, with my noble friend, who said, 'I could not give you more than ten minutes yesterday, but I will give you twenty today. I want your views about a thing which is exceedingly puzzling to me, and you are the only one to whom I like to speak on that subject. A great number of Democratic papers have been sent to me, lately, evidently written by Roman Catholics, publishing that I was born a Roman Catholic; and baptized by a priest.

"'They call me a renegade, an apostate, on account of that; and they heap upon my head mountains of abuse. At first, I laughed at that, for it is a lie, thanks be to God. I have never been a Roman Catholic. No priest of Rome has ever laid his hand on my head. But the persistency of the Romish press to present this falsehood to their readers as a gospel truth, must have a meaning. Please tell me, as briefly as possible what you think about that.'

"'My dear President,' I answered, 'it was just this strange story published about you, which brought me here yesterday. I wanted to say a word to you about it, but you were too busy. Let me tell you that I wept like a child when I read that story for the first time.

"'For, not only my impression is, that it is your sentence of death, but I have it from the lips of a converted priest, that it is in order to excite the fanaticism of the Roman Catholic murderers, whom they hope to find, sooner or later, to strike you down, they have invented that false story of your being born in the church of Rome, and of your being baptized by a priest. They want by that to brand your face with the ignominious mark of apostasy.

"'Do not forget that, in the Church of Rome, an apostate is an outcast, who has no place in society, and who has

46

no right to live. The Jesuits want the Roman Catholics to believe that you are a monster, an open enemy of God and of the church, that you are an excommunicated man.

"'I have brought to you the theology of one of the most learned and approved of the Jesuits of his time. Bussambaum, who, with many others, say that the man who will kill you will do a good and holy work. More than that, here is a copy of a decree of Gregory VII., proclaiming that the killing of an apostate, or a heretic, and an excommunicated man, as you are declared to be, is not murder; nay, that it is a good, a Christian action. That decree is incorporated in the canon law, which every priest must study, and which every good Catholic must follow.

"'My dear President. I must repeat to you here, what I said in Urbana, in 1856. My fear is that you will fall under the blows of a Jesuit assassin, if you do not pay more attention than you have done, till now, to protect yourself.

"'Remember that because Coligny was a heretic, as you are, he was brutally murdered in the St. Bartholomew night; that Henry IV. was stabbed by the Jesuit assassin, Ravaillac, the 14th of May, 1610, for having given liberty of conscience to his people, and that William, the Taciturn, was shot dead by another Jesuits murderer, called Gérard, for having broken the yoke of the Pope.

"'The Church of Rome is absolutely the same today, as she was then; she does believe and teach, today, as then, that she has the right and that it is her duty to punish with death any heretic who is in her way as an obstacle to her designs.

"'The unanimity with which the Catholic Hierarchy

of the United States is on the side of the rebels, is an incontrovertible evidence that Rome wants to destroy the Republic, and as you are—by your personal influence and popularity, your love of liberty, your position—the greatest obstacle to their diabolical scheme, their hatred is concentrated on you. You are the daily object of their maledictions; it is at your breast they will direct their blows.

"'My blood chills in my veins when I contemplate the day which may come, sooner or later, when Rome will add to all her other iniquities, the murder of Abraham Lincoln.'"

The charge that Rome was responsible for the assassination of Abraham Lincoln was first made, so far as I am advised, by Father Chiniquy; and was founded not only on the facts which I have here given, but the facts that came to him as a result of his own personal research.

His charge is distinctly and explicitly made in his book, entitled, *Fifty Years in the Church of Rome*. He there shows that Mr. Lincoln had incurred the deadly enmity of the Jesuits by foiling and disappointing them in an effort they made to convict Father Chiniquy of a crime, of which they had falsely accused him; and which, had they succeeded in convicting him, would not only have ruined his reputation, but would have secured his incarceration in prison.

Mr. Lincoln defended Father Chiniquy, and being furnished, apparently by a special Providence, with evidence that revealed their wicked conspiracy to destroy him, and convicted them of perjury, he was able, triumphantly, to defeat their wicked scheme; and gave them such a scathing as made them tremble with rage, and slink away with vows of vengeance in their hearts.

Father Chiniquy, in making his warm acknowledgements to Mr. Lincoln, could not refrain from shedding tears. Upon Mr. Lincoln's expressing surprise at this, and saying to him that he ought to be the happiest man in the world, Father Chiniquy replied, that it was for Mr. Lincoln, and not for himself, that his tears were falling.

He then explained the cause of his emotion, saying that, knowing the Jesuits as he did, and reading a purpose of vengeance in their murderous eyes, he knew that they would never rest until they had compassed his death. This occurred at Urbana, Ill., in 1856.

In the Providence of God, the duty fell on Mr. Lincoln of putting down a most formidable rebellion, and of maintaining the authority of the government by its military arm; and Father Chiniquy, realizing that a state of war would afford the Jesuits the opportunity that they sought, to at once wreak their vengeance on personal account, and give a stab at the life of the government, made three different visits to the President during his administration, to give him warning of his danger and to put him on his guard.

As Father Chiniquy has kindly give me liberty to use his book freely for the purposes of this book, I have given above the result of one of these visits, and shall make still further use of his book, in closing up this inquiry.

In doing so, however, I feel that I ought to commend Father Chiniquy's book to all who desire to inform themselves fully of the character, claims, and wicked purposed of the Roman Catholic Hierarchy. Father Chiniquy had a long, varied and cruel experience in the Roman Catholic Church; spending 25 years of his life in its priesthood.

By the grace of God he was led to see and abjure the errors of the church in which he had been reared, and so, becoming a

Christian, he has spent nearly another fifty years as an able and honored minister of the Protestant church, and in warning the nation of its danger from the Roman Catholic Hierarchy, and especially from the Jesuits.

Would that every American citizen could read his book! It would prove to him an eye opener.

8

The Most Unequivocal Proof of the Complicity of the Romish Hierarchy

We have now traced the history of this assassination as revealed by the testimony given before the Military Commission, and before a civil court, two years later; and we find ourselves coming in contact with the Roman Catholic Church, at every point, and always as a deeply interested party, thus showing its relation to the crime.

Its sympathy was always with the assassins wherever we came in contact with it. Its animus toward government was always seen to be that of the bitterest hatred and scorn; its manner that of a lion robbed of its prey.

Its every effort was to shield, and give aid to those on trial; and when it failed in this, to cast obloquy on the government, and to bring it into contempt.

Thus the history of this great crime reveals to us Rome's responsibility for the assassination of Abraham Lincoln, not as an individual man, however much of personal hatred on the part of the Jesuits might have led them to plan for his death, but as the head of the nation they desired to destroy. But we shall now proceed to give the most positive and unequivocal proof of the complicity of the Romish Hierarchy in, and its responsibility for, this crime.

Father Chiniquy was so well satisfied that the priests of Rome were at the bottom of this plot, that he spent a great deal of his time in investigating the matter, to see if he could not find convincing proof of the fact. The result of his investigations will be best given in his own words:

"'Murder will out' is a truth repeated by all nations from the beginning of the world. It is the knowledge of that truth which has sustained me in my long and difficult researches of the authors of the assassination of Lincoln, and which enables me today, to present to the world a fact, which seems almost miraculous, to show the complicity of the priests of Rome in the murder of the martyred President.

"Some time ago, I providentially met the Reverend F. A. Conwell of Chicago. Having known that I was in search of facts about the assassination of Abraham Lincoln, he told me he knew one of those facts, which might perhaps throw light on the subject of my researches.

"The very day of the murder, he said, he was in the Roman Catholic village of St. Joseph, Minnesota State, when, at about six o'clock, in the afternoon, he was told by a Roman Catholic of the place—who was a purveyor of a great number of priests who lived in that town, where they have a monastery—that the State Secretary Seward, and the President, Lincoln, had just been killed.

"'This was told me in the presence of a most respectable gentleman, called Bennett, who was not less puzzled than myself. As there were no railroad lines nearer than forty miles, nor telegraph offices nearer than eight miles, from that place, we could not see how such news was spread in that town.

"'The next day, the 15th of April, I was at St. Cloud, a town about twelve miles distant, where there are neither railroad nor telegraph. I said to several people that I had been told in the priestly village of St. Joseph, by a Roman Catholic, that Abraham Lincoln and the Secretary Seward had been assassinated, the very day before, which was Friday the 14th, at 10 o'clock p.m.

"'But how could the Roman Catholic purveyor of the priests of St. Joseph have told me the same thing, before several witnesses, just four hours before its occurrence? I spoke of that strange thing to many the same day, and the very next day I wrote to the St. Paul Press, under the head of 'A Strange Coincidence.'

"'Some time later, the editor of the St. Paul Pioneer having denied what I had written on that subject, I addressed him the following note, which he had printed, and which I have kept. Here it is; you may keep it as an infallible proof of my veracity:

To the Editor of the St. Paul Pioneer: You assume the non-truth of a short paragraph addressed by me to the St. Paul Press, viz.:

A STRANGE COINCIDENCE!
At 6:30 p.m., Friday last, April 14th, I was told as an item of news, 8 miles west of this place, that Lincoln and Seward had been assassinated. This was three hours after I had heard the news.
ST. CLOUD,
17th April, 1865.

The integrity of history requires that the above coincidence be established. And if anyone calls it in question, then proofs more ample than reared their sanguinary shadows to comfort a traitor can now be given.

Respectfully,

F. A. CONWELL.

"'I asked that gentleman if he would be kind enough to give me the fact under oath, that I might make use of it in the report I intended to publish about the assassination of Lincoln. And he kindly granted my request in the following form:

STATE OF ILLINOIS, COOK COUNTY, ss.

Reverend F. A. Conwell, being sworn deposes and says, that he is seventy-one years old; that he is a resident of North Evanston, in Cook County, State of Illinois; that he has been in the ministry for fifty-six years, and is now one of the chaplains of "Seamen's Bethel Home," in Chicago; that he was chaplain of the First Minnesota Regiment, in the war of the rebellion.

That on the 14th day of April, A.D., 1865, he was in St. Joseph, Minnesota, and reached there as early as six o'clock in the evening in company with Mr. Bennett, who, then and now, is a resident of St. Cloud, Minnesota.

That on that date, there was no telegraph nearer than Minneapolis about 80 miles from St. Joseph; and there was no railroad communication nearer than Anoka, Minnesota, about 40 miles distant.

That when he reached St. Joseph on the 14th day of April, 1865, one Mr. Linneman, who then kept the hotel of St. Joseph, told affiant that President Lincoln and Secretary Seward were assassinated; that it was not later than half past six o'clock on Friday, April 14th, 1865, when Mr. Linneman told me this.

Shortly thereafter, Mr. Bennett came into the hotel, and I told him that Mr. Linneman said the President and Secretary Seward were assassinated; and then the same Mr. Linneman reported the same conversation to Mr. Bennett in my presence.

That during that time, Mr. Linneman told me that he had charge of the friary, or college for young men, under the priests, who were studying for the priesthood at St. Joseph; that there was a number of this kind at St. Joseph at the time.

Affiant says, that on Saturday morning, April 15th, 1865, he went to St. Cloud, a distance of about 10 miles, and reached there about 8 o'clock in the morning; that there was no railroad or telegraph communication to St. Cloud.

When he arrived there he told Mr. Haworth, the hotelkeeper, that he had been told that President Lincoln and Secretary Seward had been assassinated, and asked if it was true. He further told Henry Clay Wait, Charles Gilman, who afterwards was Lieutenant Governor of Minnesota, and Reverend Mr. Tice, the same thing, and asked them if they had any such news; and they replied that they had not heard anything of the kind.

Affiant says that on Sunday morning, April 16th, 1865, he preached in St. Cloud, and on the way to the church, a copy of a telegram was handed to him, stating that the President and Secretary were assassinated on Friday evening at about nine o'clock. This telegram had been brought to St. Cloud by Mr. Gorton, who had reached St. Cloud by stage; and this was the first intelligence that had reached St. Cloud of the event.

Affiant says further, that, on Monday morning, April 17th, 1865, he furnished the 'Press', a paper of St. Paul, a statement that, three hours before the event took place, he had been informed, at St. Joseph, Minnesota, that the President had been assassinated, and this was published in the 'Press'.
(Signed)
FRANCIS ASBURY CONWELL.

Subscribed and worn to by Francis A. Conwell, before me, a Notary Public of Kankakee County, Illinois, at Chicago, Cook County, Illinois, the 6th day of September, 1883.
STEPHEN R. MOORE, Notary Public.'"

Father Chiniquy adds:

"Though this document was very important and precious to me, I felt that it would be much more valuable if it could be corroborated by the testimony of Mr. Bennett and Mr. Linneman, themselves, and I immediately sent a magistrate to find out if they were still living, and if they remembered the facts of the sworn declaration of Reverend Mr. Conwell. By the good Providence of God, both of these gentlemen were found living, and both gave the following testimonies:

STATE OF MINNESOTA, STERNS COUNTY, CITY OF ST. CLOUD, ss.
Horace B. Bennett, being sworn, deposes and says, that he is aged sixty-four years; that he is a resident of St. Cloud, Minnesota, and has resided in this county since 1856.
That he is acquainted with Reverend F. A. Conwell,

who was chaplain of the First Minnesota Regiment in the war of the rebellion.

That on the 14th day of April, 1865, he was in St. Joseph, Minnesota, in company with Mr. Frances A. Conwell; that they reached St. Joseph about sundown of said April 14th; that there was no railroad or telegraph communication with St. Joseph at that time, nor nearer than Anoka, about 40 miles distant.

That affiant, on reaching the hotel kept by Mr. Linneman, went to the barn, while Reverend F. A. Conwell entered the hotel; and shortly after affiant had returned to the hotel, Mr. Conwell had told him that Mr. Linneman had reported to him the assassination of President Lincoln; that Mr. Linneman was present and substantiated the statement:

'That on Saturday morning, April 15th, affiant and Reverend Conwell came to St. Cloud and reported that they had been told at St. Joseph about the assassination of President Lincoln.

'That no one at St. Cloud had heard of the event at this time; that the first news of the event which reached St. Cloud, was on Sunday morning, April 16th, when the news was brought by Leander Gorton, who had just come up from Anoka, Minnesota.

'That they spoke to several persons of St. Cloud concerning the matter, when they reached there, on Sunday morning, but affiant does not now remember who those different persons were, and further affiant says not.'
HORACE P. BENNETT.

Sworn before me, and subscribed in my presence, this 18th day of October. A. D., 1883.
ANDREW C. ROBINSON, Notary Public."

In regard to Mr. Linneman, Father Chiniquy says:

"Mr. Linneman, having refused to swear on his written declaration which I have in my possession, I take only from it what refers to the principal fact, viz.: that three or four hours before Lincoln was assassinated at Washington, the 14th of April, 1865, the fact was told as already accomplished in the priestly village of St. Joseph, Minnesota.

He (Linneman) remembers the time that Messrs. Conwell and Bennett came to his place (St. Joseph, Minnesota) on Friday evening, before the President was killed, and he asked them if they had heard he was dead, and they replied they had not. He heard this rumor in his store from people who came in and out. But he cannot remember from whom.

October 20th, 1883.

J. H. LINNEMAN."

9

Evidence of the Premeditated Plans
to Assassinate Abraham Lincoln

We have now before us positive evidence that these Jesuit Fathers, priests of Rome, engaged in preparing young men for the priesthood away out in the village of St. Joseph, in far off Minnesota, were in correspondence with their brethren in Washington City, and had been informed that the plan to assassinate the President had been matured, the agents for its accomplishment had been found, the time for its execution had been set, and so sure were they of its accomplishment, that they could announce it as already done, three or four hours before it had been consummated.

The anticipation of its accomplishment so elated them that they could not refrain from passing it around, in this Romish crowd, as a piece of glorious news.

It is plain from this testimony that Good Friday had been set, as the time for its accomplishment; and that ways and means had been planned, and that there was to be no such word as fail.

At the time that this news had been transmitted to these Fathers, it was not known that President Lincoln would attend

Ford's theatre; and so, it is plain that had not this opportunity been afforded to Booth and his co-conspirators, they would still have attempted it in some other way; that their purpose had been fixed; and so desperate was their determination that they would not have been foiled in their attempt by any difficulties that they might had had to encounter.

The word had been passed to this Jesuit college in St. Joseph, Minnesota, and no doubt to all other Jesuit institutions in the United States, in Canada and in the Confederacy, that, on that Good Friday, Lincoln was to be slain.

That this was to be done to overthrow our government is to be seen in the fact that Secretary Seward was also to be taken off that day.

This news could only have been communicated to these Jesuits by their Jesuit friends in Washington, who, under the protection and hospitality of our government, were thus, in the hour of its sore trial, and extreme peril, planning and plotting for its destruction: and ready, for this purpose, to resort to their favorite policy of assassination.

I feel, however that I must give my readers Father Chiniquy's own construction of this evidence. He says:

> "I present here to the world a fact of the greatest gravity, and that fact is so well authenticated that it cannot allow even the possibility of a doubt.
>
> "Three or four hours before Lincoln was murdered in Washington, the 14th of April, 1865, that murder was not only known by some one, but it was circulated and talked of in the streets, and in the houses of the priestly and Romish town of St. Joseph, Minnesota.
>
> "The fact is undeniable; the testimonies are unchallengeable, and there was no railroad or telegraph

communication nearer than 40 or 80 miles from the nearest station to St. Joseph. Naturally every one asked: 'How could such news spread? Where is the source of such a rumor?'

"Mr. Linneman, who is a Roman Catholic, tells us that, though he heard this from many in his store, and in the streets, he does not remember the name of a single one who told him that. And when we hear this from him, we understand why he did not dare to swear upon it, and shrunk from the idea of perjuring himself.

"For everyone feels that his memory cannot be so poor as that, when he remembers so well the names of the two strangers, Messrs. Conwell and Bennett, to whom he had announced the assassination of Lincoln, just seventeen years before. But if the memory of Mr. Linneman is so deficient on that subject, we can help him and tell him with mathematical accuracy.

"You got the news from your priests of St. Joseph! The conspiracy which cost the life of the martyred President was prepared by the priests of Washington in the house of Mary Surratt, No. 541 H Street.

"Those priests of Washington were in daily communication with their priests of St. Joseph; they were their intimate friends.

"There were no secrets amongst them, as there are no secrets among priests. They are the members of the same body, the branches of the same tree. The details of the murder, as the day selected for its commission, were as well known among the priests of St. Joseph as they were among those of Washington.

"The death of Lincoln was such a glorious event for those priests! The infamous apostate, Lincoln, who, baptized in the Holy Church, had rebelled against her, broken his oath of allegiance to the Pope, taken the very day of his baptism, and saved the life of an apostate!

"That infamous Lincoln, who had dared to fight against the Confederacy of the South after the Vicar of Christ had solemnly declared that their cause was just, legitimate and holy! That bloody tyrant, that godless and infamous man was to receive, at last, the just chastisement of his crimes, the 14th of April.

"What glorious news! How could the priests conceal such a joyful event from their bosom friend, Mr. Linneman?

"He was their confidential man; he was their purveyor; he was their right hand man among the faithful of St. Joseph.

"They thought that they would be guilty of a great want of confidence in their bosom friend if they did not tell him all about the glorious event that great day. But, of course, they requested him not to mention their names, if he would spread the joyful news among the devoted Roman Catholics, who, almost exclusively, formed the people of St. Joseph.

"Mr. Linneman has honorably and faithfully kept his promise never to reveal their names, and today we have in our hand the authentic testimonies, signed by him, that, though somebody on the 14th of April, told him that President Lincoln was assassinated, he does not know who told him that!

"But there is not a man of sound judgment who will have any doubt about the fact.

"The 14th of April, 1865, the priests knew and circulated the death of Lincoln four hours before its occurrence in their Roman Catholic town of St. Joseph,

Minnesota. But they could not circulate it without knowing it, and they could not know it without belonging to the band of conspirators who assassinated Abraham Lincoln."

10

Conclusion:
Appeal to the American Freeman

Our case is now before the jury of our countrymen. What say you, gentlemen? Is the charge that the Roman Hierarchy was implicated in the assassination of our martyred President sustained by the evidence which we have presented; or, has it been unjustly made?

We have no doubt of the verdict of the American people when all of this evidence, both circumstantial and positive, shall have been duly considered and weighed.

The case is too plain to admit of a reasonable doubt; and the charge of being sustained, we have before us matter for the gravest consideration; and calling for the wisest, firmest and gravest consideration; and calling for the wisest, firmest and most heroic treatment.

That same foe to our liberties—secured to us in our Constitution and Governmental institutions, that so insidiously and malignantly sought to take advantage of our civil war, which it had had a great hand in fomenting, to overthrow and destroy our government—is still in our midst; and under the guise of friendship for and love to our governmental institutions, is gaining position after position, to be used, finally, for their destruction.

There is an impending crisis, an irrepressible conflict, before us. The history of the assassination of our martyred President, which we have now before us, reveals the desperate character of the foe that we are called to face.

It is unwise to shut our eyes to the situation that confronts us. It may not be a pleasant task to contemplate the greatest of possible dangers; but it will be wiser to do so than to shut your eyes and cry peace! peace! when there is no peace.

Rome will never let go her hand, nor relax her efforts to establish her despotism until she shall have been completely despoiled of her power.

Then let the trumpet be sounded throughout the length and breadth of the land, to marshal the hosts of freedom for the conflict. Let us agitate, agitate and agitate; and then let us organize for the conflict. Let this be a war of discussion and agitation for the peaceful settlement of the great issues involved, that it may not have to be settled on the field of carnage and blood.

If it fails of the former, and much to be desired settlement, then there is but the other dreaded alternative left. It can never be a drawn battle; it will be a fight to the finish. Rome seems now to have the advantage in the contest, but it is only because the hosts of freedom are not fully awake to the issues involved.

A wily Jesuit Archbishop has had the ear of the President recently elected, and has endeavored to control his cabinet and other appointments in the interest of his church. And the patriotic people, who voted for McKinley, have expressed great disappointment at the freedom of access which the wily Jesuit has to the executive head of our nation. They have felt mortified and grieved to see him take up his quarters in Washington, and for months giving his attention to the political, rather than to the spiritual interests of his church.

They have felt that it was ominous of no good to see this Archbishop and Cardinal Gibbon cultivating such friendly relations with the President, evidently for the purpose of securing certain very desirable appointments. And they have felt disposed to censure the President for allowing this to be.

But they have no reason to find fault with the President. The Archbishop got the party down at St. Louis, when he caused the committee on platform to reject the resolutions offered to it by the representatives of the American Protective Association. The party having made this surrender to him, he felt himself to be master of the situation, and expected, of course, to have the President in his power, just as it has turned out that he has.

Neither would the case have been different had Bryan been elected. The party that nominated him would not have entertained these resolutions had they been offered in the Chicago convention; and the candidate could not have taken higher ground than his party.

It would only have been another Archbishop that would have taken him in charge, and the result would have been the same. We have, however, grounds for encouragement in the fact, now well known, that States—which the wily Jesuit had thought he had well fixed—have been smashed by the volume of protests that came to the President from all parts of the country. The patriotic orders were weak in the convention, but strong in protests.

It becomes us now to consider the cause of their weakness in the convention. Their weakness did not lie in lack of numbers, but in the want of an organization. The vote of the various patriotic orders in the United States outnumbers the Roman Catholic vote by at least three to one; and yet it was the Roman

Catholic vote that could command the consideration of the political leaders of the land.

It is easy to see why this was the case. The thorough organization of the forces of the Hierarchy is well understood. It is known that this vote can be wielded, virtually, as a unit by the priesthood, and that it can be secured by whichever party makes the highest bid for it. It is thought to be a balance of power vote in a presidential election, and the priests desire to have it so considered, in order to secure the highest price for it; not in cash, but in place and power.

This is the secret of Rome's power with the politicians.

And now the question of prime importance is, how is this power to be broken?

It can only be done by a compact and thorough organization of the entire patriotic vote of the country. This vote is sufficiently large to control the entire situation; but is powerless in its present disorganized condition.

It is vain to think of gaining the victory over Rome through either of the two dominant parties. They have gotten so demoralized, through long subservience to Rome, and know so well the power of its organization, and have so little dread of the patriotic organizations in their present scattered and disjointed condition, that nothing short of a crushing defeat will ever cause them to follow the dictates of patriotism.

It will take a new party. The flame of patriotism must be aroused to the height of a sublime endeavor. Men must be taught to follow the flag, rather than party.

We must have a party that will boldly take its stand on a platform of American fundamental principles. It must declare for the immediate incorporation of the XVIth Amendment into our National and State Constitutions. This will settle, for good, the question of the appropriation of public funds to any sectarian purposes whatsoever, and secure the complete separation of the Church and State.

It must also declare for such amendments to our emigration laws as will exclude all undesirable classes from coming to our shores: such as criminals, paupers, illiterates, vicious, and all who are in any way disqualified for making good and desirable American citizens.

Then, to those admitted, the limit of their probation must be extended to such a length of time as is necessary to enable them to become acquainted with the nature and to catch the spirit of our institutions.

The right to vote must be based upon a qualification of intelligence.

The rightful jurisdiction of the civil power must be exercised over all private institutions in which people are held under surveillance and control for the preservation of the rights and liberties of their inmates.

No property held by any religious society, other than actual houses of worship, should be exempt from taxation.

Now, whatever party can rise to the highest of these requirements for the protection of our institutions, and will incorporate these measures in its platform, should receive the undivided support of the American Protective Association (APA), and of all of the other patriotic organizations, and individual citizens; provided, that in connection with these, it shall embrace all other reforms in our policy that are essential to the prosperity of our country.

A party that is sound in its Americanism, and patriotic in its purposes, may be safely trusted to find, ultimately, the right side of all other questions.

The People's party ought, in addition to its other reform measures, to be able to arise to the height of these requirements;

but it will perhaps be found to be too much under the influence of the politicians, who seem to think that to set themselves against the Romish Hierarchy would be fatal to the success of any party.

It will, in all probability, be found necessary to organize the patriotic forces into a new party, that will have the courage to accept, and to meet the issues presented fairly and squarely; and to take the name that logically presents itself: "The Protestant American Party."

Our civil institutions are the logical outcome of the protest of Luther and his co-adjutors against the Papal despotism. They are but the garnered fruit of the tree of the Reformation. The foe we have to fight is the same that they had to contend against.

The contention is in a part, at least, over the same issues; for it is the civil claims of the Papacy, and not its religious dogmas, that we are, in the present field of operations, called upon to resist.

These latter we accord to it the right to hold, and to teach; believing with Jefferson that "error is harmless whilst truth is left to combat it;" so, that, however erroneous and soul-destroying we may think its dogmas to be, they must still be held to be under the domain of reason, and to be overthrown by truth; and so, not under civil control.

But the claim of the Papacy to supreme civil jurisdiction must be met, according to its nature, in the field of politics.

To admit this claim is to surrender all human rights, and human liberty, to the keeping of a fallible fellow-mortal; and to enthrone him as a despot. This is what is done in theory by every loyal son of the church of Rome; and to bring all mankind into the same bondage with himself is ever to be his supreme endeavor.

Every Roman Catholic priest, of whatever grade, believes the Pope to be Christ's vicar on earth, and to stand to the human race, in all matters, spiritual and temporal, in the place of God. This places him in the position of supreme authority; so that all civil power must be dispensed under his direction and control.

Every priest not only believes this, but is put under the obligation of his oath of ordination to use all the means that may at any time be in his power to bring the whole world into the acceptance of this dogma, and to submission to the Pope's authority.

This is what the whole body of the Romish priesthood in the United States are engaged in today; and it means the subjugation of our Protestant civil institutions, and the surrender of our liberties. Here we have Romanism pitted against Protestantism, and its success simply means the destruction of our government, and the enthronement over us of the Prince of all Despots.

Let us then have the courage to take a name that immediately suggests the issues involved in the contest, and the nature of the contention, and thus raise a banner that will draw to its support every lover of liberty, and foe of despotism.

Nothing would more alarm the foe we have to fight than this party name, that would so clearly indicate the real matter at issue; and nothing would more cheer and encourage the hosts of freedom.

I am aware that this proposition will be met with the objection that it would be unwise and dangerous to introduce the element of religious differences into our political contests, and especially, to make this the basis of party organizations.

But it is sufficient to meet this objection with the simple truth, that it is the civil claims of the Romish Hierarchy that we resist; and these come clearly under the domain of politics.

In this resistance we do not interfere with, or even call in question, the Papal system of religion. Every American citizen, who had had his mind expanded with the Protestant ideas of civil and religious liberty, will ever stand ready to accord to his Roman Catholic fellow citizens the same right to protection in their rights of conscience, in matters of religion, that he claims for himself; but he will at the same time see to it, that under the guise of religion, he shall not be allowed to undermine the very foundation of these privileges.

Our country must be maintained as it is now, the land of liberty, under the protection of Protestant institutions. Let us then declare to the world this purpose, by bringing it under the control of a "Protestant American Party."

The Hierarchy has never had to encounter anything in this country that has given it so much concern as does the present patriotic awakening.

It affects, however, to regard it with contempt, but at the same time redoubles its efforts to tighten its grasp on the politicians. It is to them that it looks for help, and appeals for aid.

It tries to hide the real issues, by its usual resort to misrepresentation and falsehood. It represents it as a revival of know-nothingism. In this it is not so far wrong.

The APA is, however, built on a broader foundation, as a result of a wider knowledge, and more extended experience of the deadly hostility of Rome to our civil institutions; and so upon a better comprehension of the safeguards that are necessary for the protection.

It represents this, and all the other patriotic organizations, as founded on bigotry and for the purpose of religious persecution; and so, as being un-American and unpatriotic.

And all this is to throw chaff into the eyes, that they may be closed to the threatened danger.

But in this way, many well-meaning people and true friends of our institutions, and lovers of our country's flag, are being deceived, and lulled to sleep.

Now, why does Rome resort to this line of defense? It is because all of the facts are against her, and so, as they cannot be denied or controverted, her policy is to hide them out of sight, by changing the line of vision.

Rome knows, and every American citizen ought to know, that these anti-Catholic agitators are unearthing her purposes, and uncovering her plans to get hold of all the departments of our Government, to then give to the Pope all that he claims as Christ's vicar—supreme control over our civil institutions— that he may wield the civil power for the upbuilding of the so-called church. We have only to turn to the pages of history to learn how he would use this power.

We want no more of his interference with our God-given rights. We want no more union of church and state; and the danger lies, more than anything else, in the seeming incredibility that there should be any persons found at this late day, and in this land of ours, who would favor a return to the rack, the thumbscrews, and other instruments of inquisition torture, for the promotion of the glory of God, and the salvation of souls.

Let the incredulous look at Rome's boasted declaration: *Semper eadem*; let them also scan the declarations made by Romish priests of every grade, in recent years, in the Roman Catholic Journals and Periodicals; and they will learn that all that Rome wants is the power to enable her to revive these mild methods of propagating her version of the Gospel of Christ.

Why doesn't she meet the charges that are made against her openly and fairly?

When it is charged that she is storing away arms in the basements of her churches, why does she not proffer the keys, and invite inspection?

When it is charged that she is restraining helpless females of their liberty, for the basest purposes, and inflicting upon them untold cruelties to bring them under subjection to a lecherous, drunken priesthood, why does she not open her doors, and appeal to the civil magistrates to make the most rigid inspection and examination, that they may thus show the charges to be false?

This she has never yet done, and never will do; neither will she permit it to be done as long as she can find means for successful resistance.

In the name of liberty, in the cause of humanity, let us compel her to submit to such inspections. In the name of Protestant Americanism, let us set up our banners for complete subjugation of this corrupt, unscrupulous, and dangerous foe to liberty, and murderer of human rights.

Let it be known to the world that American freemen will ever stand on the watch tower, and will compel the submission of all within the domain of our government to submit themselves to its rightful authority. That there can be in this country in civil affairs no power greater than the State.

Printed in the USA
CPSIA information can be obtained
at www.ICGtesting.com
LVHW091615311023
762671LV00006B/198